<u>IMPOSSIBLE IS POSSIBLE WITH GOD</u>

Zamazulu Nomcebo Mncwango

<u>COPYRIGHT</u>

CONTENTS

<u>SPECIAL ACKNOWLEDGEMENTS</u>

To my late Granny 'Mirriet Masondo'

Granny, thank you for instilling the love and the fear of God in me. You taught me the importance and power of prayer. You gave me the best gift of life anyone can ask for - God's unconditional love. Ngiyabonga Gogo, ngiyohleze ngikuthanda! ☺' I love you grandmother and I will always love you'.

---------- /\ ----------

To my late mom – Gloria T.Mncwango'

I loved you then and I still love you now. You were the most beautiful, kind, caring, considerate, straight forward, very driven, independent and loving human being, who was loved by many. There are times when I miss you so much and I wish you were still here with me alive and well. There is so much I wanted to do for you, to show my gratitude and my love for you. I'm thankful for the 25 years of my life that I spent with you. I have many beautiful memories of you that I will cherish forever. You taught me so much and all that has helped me to be the woman I am today. The hard work, the achievements and the woman I am today, I hope you're proud of me. I will always love you, mama 'mother'.

---------- /\ ----------

To my dad - 'BJ Mncwango'

Thank you for your teachings, your love, support and for all the sacrifices you made for me. You were very strict on me and I did not get it until just a few years ago that you being strict on me was the best thing you did for me because it has helped me be the strong and independent woman that I am today.

To my Fiancé - 'Bheki Godfrey Shabangu'

Thank you for making this journey possible. Thank you for your unwavering support throughout this experience. Thank you for showing me that together, we can overcome anything. Thank you for the person that you are, I appreciate you so much, you are such a blessing. This experience brought us closer than before and we came out victorious, we are more than conquerors. I Love you s'thandwa sami 'my love ' with all my heart.

My Daughter – 'Nokukhanya Destiny Mncwango'

Thank you for being my 'nana' child. Your love and understanding from the beginning gave me confidence that Manqoba will pull through. You have been a source of inspiration, young as you are, thank you for making parenthood a pleasure by just being you. I love you, 'nana' child! May you grow and realize what God has called you to be. May you be your best self that you wish to be. May God keep you safe and His goodness and mercy follow you all the days of your life.

Special dedication – To my son

'Manqoba (Conquer)Smangaliso (Miracle)Shabangu'

I dedicate this book to my son, my miracle from God. Every time I look at you, I see God's wonder, God's love, God's grace, God's answer to my prayers. You fought a good fight of faith, you wrestled with and conquered death. You came out victorious. UnguManqoba ngempela 'You are a true Conqueror'. UyiSmangaliso sikaJehovah ngempela 'You are God's miracles'. Nothing shall be impossible for you in this life. I declare God's favour today and beyond. I declare you're blessed. You shall live to see and experience God's supernatural providence upon your life. May you live to become that which God has called you to be

Manqoba, I hope one day you will realize that, you are carrying something big inside of you, a special anointing, a special gift which does not give the devil peace. Whatever it is that God has deposited in you, is greater than we can imagine. Only time will tell. Only time will reveal to us.

May He grant me the wisdom, strength, patience and all that I will need to help you get to your destiny. Whatever challenges you will face as you grow older and older, may you be reminded of your inner strength, may this book remind you what a conqueror you are and that you can do all things through Christ who gives you strength.

May God's goodness and mercy follow you all the days of your life.

Love you my handsome boo-boo 'son'.

SPECIAL DEDICATION TO YOU (THE ONE READING THIS BOOK)

I dedicate this book to all the women who lost their babies during birth, those who gave birth prematurely and those who overcame all challenges. I do not leave out all the men who have been supportive to their partners through any challenges they went through; giving birth, losing a child, raising a child with disability or special needs.

I also dedicate this book to any person under the sun who is going through hardships right now. I want to remind you through this book that; you can tell your mountain to move and it shall move. You can conquer anything with God by your side. It is not over until God says it is over. Do not give up, do not throw in the towel. You are not alone, He is with you every step of the way, just trust Him. Do not kill yourself. God has great plans for you, plans to prosper you and not to harm you, plans to give you hope and a future.

May the testimonies in this book give you hope and strengthen you through your journey.

OVERVIEW

Pregnancy is a time of many changes. Your body, your emotions, your life and, the life of your family changes. Your body goes through mental and physical stages before and during pregnancy; some of which I was not prepared for. Having a baby is a huge life changing experience.

You may welcome these changes, but they can add new stresses (good or not so good) to your life.

Pregnancy is a journey, and quite honestly, something that I never thought I would experience. It is a miraculous blessing to be able to carry a baby and I am so very thankful for our sweet little boy, Manqoba. My pregnancy presented many challenges, but I will spare you from ALL the details for now.

WHO AM I?

My name is Zamazulu in short Zama which means 'Try' Nomcebo 'Teasure' Mncwango, a Zulu girl, born in KwaNongoma, in Kwa-Zulu Natal, South Africa. I grew up in Vryheid, raised by my granny for the first six years of my life. I was just a granny's baby. I relocated to Johannesburg in 1993 to stay with my parents.

I am a very friendly and kind person, who loves people and to help them where I am able to help. I am very protective of myself; I love my private space. Within my space, I love having people I can trust, those who will be loyal to me, just as much as I will be loyal to them.

My beliefs

I am a child of God. I am where I am today because of Him. God has been good to me and I am not ashamed to declare that I serve a living God who will never leave me nor forsake me. He is my protector, my healer, my comforter and my provider. He is my everything.

My family

I am a daughter, a sister, a friend, a colleague, a mother of two children, a beautiful teenage girl and a handsome and adorable baby boy and I am a fiancée to my loving partner.

My career

I am a Radio personality in the number one community radio station in South African – (Jozi FM, 105.8 stereo). I present a prime-time slot in the mornings between 9am till 12 midday weekdays. I'm a DJ, an MC, an Inspirational speaker, a Business woman, an Author, a Fashion designer just to name a few. There is so much I still want to venture into, watch the space.

Life motto

Take care of the inner self and your outer self, will glow. I believe God created me for a purpose. He has blessed me with many diverse gifts. I am here to serve my time and use these gifts to His glory. I need wisdom to serve God and glorify Him. This is my time and I will use it to my level best to be everything God created me to be.

1. THE HIJACKING EXPERIENCE

Fear not, for I am with you, be not dismayed,
for I am your God. I will strengthen you,

Yes, I will help you, I will uphold you with my
righteous right hand

Isaiah 41:10

Words of inspiration

Never doubt God, always believe in Him, His plan is always the best, sometimes the process may be hard and painful but He will carry you through, just trust Him.

In September 2017, I suspected that I might be pregnant because I missed my monthly period. It didn't come as a surprise because we had discussed it with my partner and he had asked that we try for a baby. It just happened sooner than we expected. We did a pregnancy test and it confirmed that I was pregnant. I experienced mixed emotions about it, my eldest daughter was almost 15 years, and somehow, it felt like the first, I had forgotten about mothering an infant, it was a bit of scary feeling but again, a little bit of excitement. Before I could make sense of my emotions, we had an experience.

On the 12th October 2017, on a Thursday, which is one of my favourite days at work, its a Gospel Edition show, powered by gospel music, a pastor, a gospel artist, basically it's a show all about drawing closer to God. I enjoyed the whole 4 hours of the show, as per usual, then went home. Mind you, I had started feeling some symptoms as part of the pregnancy, feeling tired and sleepy. On this day, my partner came home to see me just before 9pm and he was not going to stay for long because he was very tired after a long day at work. He asked for something to drink and I prepared some juice and we had a chat in the car which he had just bought, three weeks ago. While we were chatting, we heard rough knocks on the windows on both sides of the car, these guys pointing guns at us and pointed us out of the front sit to the back of the car.

It felt like a nightmare, like it was just a bad dream, BUT it was all so real. It all happened around 8:50pm. They instructed us not to look at them, they took our phones and our watches. They asked if the car had a tracker and whether my partner had a gun. They then drove around with us for a few minutes then they stopped and asked us to get out of the car. I remember seeing my fiancé, they were holding him so tight they then put us inside another car, but my fiancé was instructed to go into the boot because they feared that he might fight them. For about three hours, they were just driving around with us in the car. I was terrified, many thoughts ran through my head, one of them being; 'what if they rape me then kill us?' Weird enough, at some point my fiancé was also fearing the same thing.

He was worried about me, he kept calling my name from the boot and asking if I was okay, they assured us that they will not hurt us, they are just doing their job, and will drop us off somewhere safe, they just needed us to cooperate. I did not know whether to believe them or not, only God knew how all this will end.

I remember at some point, as they were talking amongst themselves, in my mind and in my spirit, I was singing gospel songs that comforted me and calmed me down and at that time I knew God will protect us. I believed our situation will be different from the ones we would hear of, on both radio and television.

We continued driving around with the one guy as if he was looking for somebody or a location. I suspected the guy was new in this whole gang thing, he kept talking to me and reassuring me they will not hurt us. He kept saying I must not look at him, at that time, my partner was still in the boot and he would reassure him as well that they are just doing their job and they will not hurt us. Every now and then as we were still in the car, my partner would ask if I was okay, and the guy finally asked; why he keeps asking you if you're okay? I told him I was pregnant. Amazingly he became even more kind to me. There was a time he even offered me juice or snacks, that's when he passed by his girlfriend's place. At one point he was telling me about his child and even suggested a name for my unborn child 'uLwandle' which means 'Ocean' can you believe it!

I remember it got to a point where I needed to use the bathroom. You know as a 'preggie' woman, this will come. I told him I needed to relief myself and he said he would look for a place that's more quiet so I can relief myself and we got to a place which was very quiet, there was no one in the street and I got out of the car and relieved myself, right next to the car. At that time, I had moved to the front sit because the two guys had taken our car to go hide it. We drove again until the two guys were done hiding the car then we went to fetch them.

After some time driving around with all three guys they dropped us off at Booysens. It was already mid-night. You could hear that they are used to doing this job. They use a coded language, call places by numbers. We got to the place which they agreed on. They stopped the car and released my partner and instructed him to walk into a near-by veld and he must not look back. They gave me his leather jacket which they were fighting over because the one guy wanted it, while the other one wanted me to get the jacket to keep warm. So, I wore the jacket and they instructed me to get out of the car as well and follow my fiancé in the veld. Then they drove off.

It was passed midnight, since they took us before 9pm, it was freezing cold, we walked trying to find our way. We got to one factory and saw a security guard who helped us after explaining what had happened. He helped us send a 'PLS Call' back to one of our relatives, who then called back and we told him what had happened. We then continued walking, looking for a petrol station and eventually found one. Whilst still there, police passed by and my partner ran to them and told them about the whole ordeal.

They drove us to Orlando Police Station, Soweto to open a case. We learnt that the Ford Ranger was one of the kinds of cars on the hit list. I remember, as we drove on the freeway with the two policemen, we saw somebody gunned down. We found out few days later via the news that the person was hijacked, killed and dropped off in the freeway. You know finding out about such news, makes you appreciate life, knowing we survived a similar kind of a situation.

The car was still new, my partner had not even memorised the registration. I know for him, this was his achievement, he had just bought that car, so it was not easy at all for him. We got home around 3am, we were exhausted and went to bed, however, we could not fall asleep, I had flashbacks from the hijacking experience.

More than anything else, from the experience, one thing I learned and acknowledged was that God was with us in that ordeal. I saw God in that situation. We are thankful that we came out alive. He protected us.

Manqoba survived and overcame this ordeal in my womb. Few days afterwards, we went for the first scan, seeing his little body and hearing his heart beat, I moved from being a little scared to being expectant of meeting this little person inside of me.

Even though the car was never found, what is important is life. We are grateful to be alive and to be able to testify and give witness about God's greatness. Many get raped or even killed in a hijacking. We lived to tell our story.

For some time, I would still feel terrified and traumatized. I was still living in the same area; I would lock the gate early than usual and lock the doors as well. We never went for counselling instead we chose to talk about the incident amongst ourselves and at times we would go for a drive at night as a way of healing ourselves.

Have we healed from that incident? Mmmh, I'm not sure especially on my partner's side. We are taking it one day at a time. Nonetheless, we thank God for our lives. He definitely showed Himself on our behalf throughout this ordeal.

2. <u>GOD WILL NEVER GIVE YOU MORE THAN WHAT YOU CAN HANDLE</u>

For I know the plans I have for you, declares the Lord, plans to prosper you and not harm you, plans to give you hope and a future

Jeremiah 29:11

Words of Inspiration

God will never give you more than what you can handle.
He knows you because you are His child,

and He has trusted you. He knows you can conquer the mountain.

Whatever situation you face in life, it is important to understand that God trusts you with it, no matter how small or big. The important thing is to trust in Him and call on Him for help. You need to understand that He will never leave you nor forsake you. He will do just what He said in His Word. This is what He did for us. We called on Him and trusted Him throughout the ordeal. He delivered us. He heard us and He answered our prayers.

Today, we are able to talk and share about our testimony, our journey where the Lord carried us through. It was by His grace and mercy that we made it, that Manqoba made it. All glory to God. He is a faithful and good God.

Life lessons

Out of the ordeal, I took some life lessons. I got to learn the importance of making life decisions. I am one person who would normally procrastinate taking action on some of the plans I needed to execute. After this ordeal, I decide that NO MORE DELAYS IN MY LIFE moving forward.

I execute whatever it is I intend to do. I am more focused. I actually got to understand that we don't know how much time we have on earth; we need to do what God has called us to do, give it our all, our best, with no excuses. I am driven to live my life purposefully now more than ever before.

Make or break

From the ordeal, I also observed that it brought me and my partner closer than we were before. Such a situation can truly make or break you as a couple. In our case, it brought us closer, it strengthened our love, our belief and confidence in God than ever before. That situation, on our own, we would not have made it. We believe more in God than we did before. Our faith in God has been increased and strengthened.

3. <u>MY PREGNANCY JOURNEY</u>

But the angel said to her, do not be afraid, Mary, you have found favour with God. You will be with a child and give birth to a son...

Luke 1:30-31

Words of Inspiration

Give thanks for all He has done for you, small or big.

That which you can see and that of the spiritual eyes.

He does not sleep nor does He rest,

He is working things in your favour.

He hears your prayers and it's only a matter of time before He answers you.

Be patient, it will happen, it's going to happen.

My 'preggie' journey was smooth and enjoyable, never experienced morning sickness or any other complications. I only experienced fatigue in the first trimester due to body changes and adjustments. Just knowing there is a little person growing inside of me, obviously came with changes; change in diet, eating carefully, drinking lots of water and taking a walk to and from work as a way of exercising as well and making sure I rested more. I just did everything right; I mean according to the book. I was enjoying the journey.

Support system

I had all the support I needed. My fiancé was incredibly supportive; he was there all the way. My family was supportive. My daughter as well, especially when I had told her we are expecting, she was hoping it would be a little sister. We in fact, hoped it would be twins since we have the twin gene in our family. Nonetheless, we were happy to have this bundle of joy, the young man called Manqoba Smangaliso Shabangu as an additional member to our family.

A boy or girl

I was not really keen in knowing the baby's gender, I actually wanted to be surprised at birth. One morning, as I was preparing to go to work, I realised I was 'spotting', little red blood stains and as a heavily 7th month pregnant woman, I got worried because it is something that is not supposed to happen, lest there is some risk or something gone wrong or even some complications. Immediately, I called the midwife where I was attending antenatal classes, and I was told to go straight to the consulting rooms for a thorough check up.

When the midwife conducted the check-up, she confirmed everything was fine, the baby's heartbeat was normal, but she referred me to another doctor, for another appointment which was in few more days to come. My fiancé felt we could not and should not wait till then, we decided to go see a Gynaecologist at a Private Hospital and the doctor said it was just a discharge and will prescribe some medication and all should be back to normal.

The doctor did a scan just to confirm that everything was fine with the baby. He then mentioned that we will be having a baby boy… *Ooooohh!* There goes my surprise, our surprise. I didn't want to know the baby's gender as yet, but what can I say?

 Anyway, I left knowing that we are going to have a baby boy.

Post baby gender 'revelation'

I started on the medication given to heal this 'spotting'. The following day, the spotting still continued, but since I was on medication, I thought it will stop. My partner and I went to Vaal, he had a project he was working on. On our way there, I began to feel some discomfort, feeling pains like menstrual pains. I thought they would go away, took my medication, but instead the pains continued and got worse. I made my partner aware that the pain was not normal because they were not stopping. They were becoming unbearable.

We asked around for a clinic nearby. On arrival at the clinic, I explained my condition and was given some more tablets and told I should be alright. We left the clinic hopeful. However, these pains were not getting any better, they actually got worse. My partner took me home to rest, hoping everything will be OK. BUT the pains grew severe, on both sides, my back and my lower abdomen. I was now seriously worried and by that time, my partner had gone back to Vaal.

So, I called him and told him I think I might be in labour, the pains were severe and it felt like contractions. I truly felt like I was going to give birth. I also called my midwife and she advised I get to the hospital immediately.

The pains were seriously hectic, I realised I was in labour and the urge to push was real. I was with my daughter at home, there was no way I could give birth at home, it was too risky. I breathed as much as I could. My partner arranged with one of his employee to come take me to hospital, he arrived and drove insanely fast, rushing me to the hospital, upon arrival, I just had the urge to push. Just when we got to the casualty section, I felt I could no longer hold myself any longer, I started pushing and my bundle of joy, my baby boy landed. I gave birth to a beautiful baby boy. It all happened so fast.

My baby boy was born on the 9th March 2018. Yes, it may have been earlier than expected, but I was glad to hold him in my arms and officially welcomed him to this world.

4. <u>BEFORE TIME OR ON TIME?</u>

A time for everything. There is a time for everything, and a season for every activity under the Heavens. A time to be born and a time to die' Ecclesiastes 3:1-2

Words of Inspiration

When I went for my first scan to the doctor, he estimated I would give birth around May??

I also thought it would be in May 2018, although I was not sure about the date, we could not be more wrong. I gave birth to our beautiful baby boy on the 9th March 2018 at 6:10 in the evening.

It was not in the doctor's time, and certainly not in my time, but in God's time. His time is the right time.

Whatever is happening in your life right now, it's the time for it to happen because we go through seasons in our lives, like we go through seasons year in and year out on this earth.

Birth at 7 months

I gave birth to my son at 6:10pm, in the 7th month of pregnancy which was something I didn't expect since everything was going well with the pregnancy. The nurse gave me his little body to hold for probably 2-5 seconds and took him away. The doctors came, took him and they were busy with him, for about 30 minutes or more, they were just busy with him. I was taken care of by another nurse, but my mind, my eyes were on my boy.

I kept asking if he was fine and the nurse assured me that he was. They are attending to him, just breathing challenges and since he was born prematurely, he will be kept in the Intensive Care Unit (ICU). I didn't get to see him that whole Friday evening, until the following morning.

I was happy that he was alive and well. His dad came to check up on us. He was happy to hear that the little man was ok. He had bought him clothes and other necessities. Imagine, we had not gone shopping because we thought there was still more time before his birth. I was planning to have a photo shot whilst pregnant but I never got that chance. That is how Manqoba came into this world.

I remember when I got to the ward, where he was laid, all I could see was the machine, making that beeping sound. The nurse helped me to find my son. I knew it was him because I had seen his face, I had marked his face. I looked at him in that machine, with a huge pipe in his nose, going across his face to the back. It was the scariest thing I have ever seen. I cried, I cried and left the ward. It was just too much for me. Few minutes later, I went back in again. I realized I had to be strong for my baby. His dad came in and saw him for the first, we had not decided on the names but as we were there in ICU, his dad said "You will conquer my son and then he said uManqoba and I said "He is a miracle from God and God will do miracles in his life and that's how his names came about. Manqoba meaning to conquer and Smangaliso meaning miracle. These are prophetic names, we were already declaring that our son will make it, he will conquer because he is God's miracle to us and to the world.

Hospital stay

Manqoba was in hospital for 1month and 11 days. That was the longest month in my entire life. He went through so much. Where do I start?

- *Breathing:* He was on a breathing machine, he was struggling to breath independently, he needed oxygen pipe to help him.
- *Eating:* He was also eating through a small pipe.

He was moved out of the ICU and put in another ward because his condition was improving. I was there in the hospital, daily from 7am until 6pm, spending time with him. His dad would come join us during visiting hours.

Daily, I would pray for him, asking God to miraculously heal him. I would declare the Lord's healing power over his tiny body, from the head to the little toes. As parents, we took authority, we stood in agreement, prayed for him, embrace him, touch him on both sides and cry out to God to heal him. Day after day, we saw him improve, he was removed from the pipe machine. This time around, the pipe was changed to a smaller one.

He was put in Section C because his condition was improving. He weighed 1.7kg, it was not scary small because he seemed bigger compared to other babies in the ward. It was not nice having him at the hospital, leaving him every night. BUT, we kept trusting the Lord that Manqoba will make it. He will pull through all the challenges. He will overcome, just like his name professes.

Fatal human error

It would serve as common sense that a baby born prematurely needs to be kept in an incubator, but this was not the case with my son. He was never placed in an incubator when he was born and this was an error by a nurse. I recall when I got to the hospital, the machine was off and I made the nurse who was present at the time aware about this. She was rude towards me; told me she was busy with another baby who had a more serious case to deal with. She ignored me and never attended to the machine. I even left that day after 6 in the evening with that machine still off.

The following morning, I realised the machine was still not switched on. I picked up my baby and realise he was cold, stone cold. His body was cold and he was weak. Fortunately, the doctor arrived for normal routine check-up. She picked him up, realised my baby was cold, which was something that should not be. She called for an incubator. They brought something that looked like a plastic bag to cover my baby and to warm him up.

I realize this error of misjudgement, of negligence from the nurse could have cost my dear son's life. I was so angry at her because of how casually she was when my son's life was at risk. I blamed her for all that happened, she gave me a bad attitude, an attitude that almost cost my son's life. I got so angry towards her, and didn't want to converse or relate with her. She eventually came and apologised. I forgave her and focused on my son and his recovery. Days passed by, he was then out of ICU into normal ward, Ward 66.

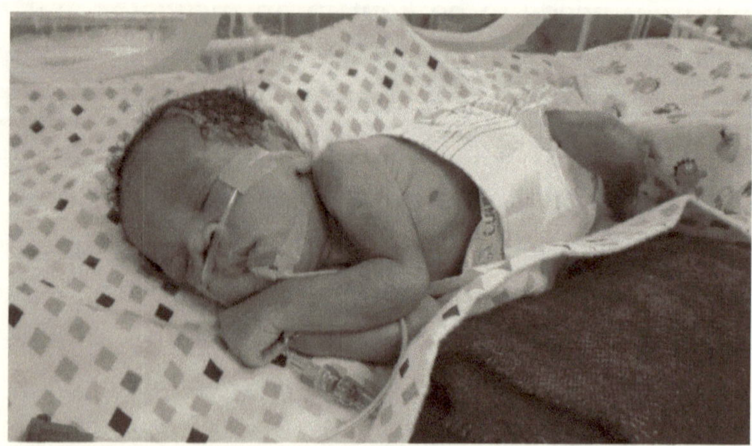

Ward 66

Manqoba was moved to Ward 66 where I witnessed that his condition kept on improving steadily. One day he was just crying non-stop and uncontrollably. I did all the basics that needed to be done, either he is hungry, needed nappy change or wanted to sleep. None of those were of concern or the cause. Then I realised his feet were swollen, they looked different from the day before and his belly was looking different than it was usually. I told the *other* nurse who just casually told me nothing was wrong with my son. She came to check on him and still maintained that nothing was wrong.

This is the second time now a nurse misjudges my son's condition for attention seeking. I could not shake off the feeling that he is not fine. I left the nurse and went straight to the Matron. She came to see my son and I explain what was going on and she checked my son and saw the need to call a doctor to come and again the doctor checked him. He confirmed that Manqoba had an infection. Once again, the motherly instinct was spot on. I was correct that something was not right. My heart was broken, I could not believe the negligence and carelessness of the nurse, especially when you raise a concern about your baby who is admitted in a hospital ward. Another episode to deal with, my baby had another battle to overcome.

On his healing journey

I guess we had to go through all of this *again*, it was another blow but we believed God for his complete healing. Our faith remained steadfast; we didn't have any other choice. We needed divine intervention. I managed to gather strength and spoke to the nurse who ignored my call for her attention. She acknowledged she was wrong about my son then, and she apologised about the incident.

It was never easy being in the hospital. It was not easy at all. I would find myself crying and crying silently, because of the things that happened there, having to go every day to visit, to check, to see my baby. Nonetheless, I continued to pray to God to heal him so we can take him home where he will grow well and be taken care of. I refused to believe otherwise. I knew God will come through for all of us.

Section C vs the ICU

One of the things that made me appreciate ward 66 compared to ICU was that, in ICU, I could not bond with my baby but in the ward, I could hold him, the kangarooing way. This means holding my baby in my chest, skin-to-skin contact. This I was told, helps the baby to grow faster and gives the baby peace of mind, they are close to your heart, and to the baby, it is like the similar 'environment' as inside the womb. I was told it was good for my baby. I would do that for hours, day in and day out. It felt so good because I felt so close to him and it helped build and strengthen the bond between us. uSmangaliso kept growing stronger and became better and better daily.

While in Ward 66, he would be taken for routine check-ups, this was to monitor his heart because he had a hole in his heart at birth. Once in a while, he needed to be taken to the ECHO ROOM to check if this hole was closing up or not. Another condition he was diagnosed with, which I was never informed nor was never explained to me. I was told by a doctor, one day when we went for a head scan that the bleeding in his brain is slowing down. This was a shock to me, I never knew there was bleeding in his brain. It came as a shock. I was never told that my son had a bleeding problem in his brain. Now, I discovered that it was improving. I didn't know how to react. I was dumbstruck. My heart was broken AGAIN. All along I knew about the hole in his heart, but the bleeding in his brain, I didn't know what that truly meant for his condition. This was emotionally draining and strenuous.

My son being in hospital was the most awful, dreadful and stressful time, a nightmare in my life, with some days better than others, whilst many of those were worse. I continued to pray to God, and still believed God will come through for my son and for us as his family. I refused to give up hope. I realized this was a mountain I needed to be ready to climb.

Emotional support and pillar of strength

I was becoming emotionally weak; I would cry whenever I heard bad news. It was just too much. Seeing a helpless little human being having to go through all this, it was unfair. After talking to his dad, I would feel like my strength was coming back. He didn't express his true emotions about the whole experience. He wanted to be strong for me, he wanted to be a pillar of strength for me but it was harder for him to break down and express his emotions. He focused on helping me to be strong, he kept reassuring me that our boy will make it and come out of the hospital well. He would affirm me that God will answer our prayers.

Manqoba was kept in ward 66, with continuous improvement. I remember, there was this one nurse in the ward, she was a grown elderly woman. I loved her attitude, she was very nice, had a beautiful heart, she was a blessing. She possessed such a positive spirit which was something I truly needed during this ordeal. She was a God-sent in that ward especially for me and my son. She stood out from amongst the ward staff. She would speak and release an encouraging word, she would advise that we go to church and get our spirits lifted up, and pray for our babies, and she will look after them in our absence. I will never forget that nursing sister. God knew what I needed and He provided through her. Do you remember that programme on TV called 'Touched by an angel'? She was that angel that touched our lives.

I remember one time we went for Manqoba's heart check-up, she said she will not put him on an oxygen machine because we trusted God will enable him to breath independently. The slight testing period seemed to be working well, the doctors were even surprised. Manqoba was going for about an hour to two, breathing independently. The doctor even said it looked positive that the baby might be discharged earlier than expected. Manqoba did exceptionally well breathing on his own. He was put back again onto the oxygen machine just so he does not get exhausted.

He kept fighting a good fight. He was responding to the faith we had in God about his recovery. He kept showing signs of victory daily. This was encouraging to us as his parents.

5. <u>POEM - 'KEEP MOVING'</u>

He says; those who hope in the Lord will renew their strength. They will soar on wings like eagles; they will run and not grow weary. They will walk and not be faint.

Isaiah 40:31

Words of Inspiration

Whatever situation you in, let God be your refuge and strength. Let Him be your help in trouble, as much as it may be scary, hard even painful being in that

situation, do not fear. He says in Isaiah 46 :4 "Even to your old age, I am He, and even to grey hairs I will carry you! I have made, and I will bear; even I will carry and will deliver you.

Poem

<u>"Keep Moving"</u>

By Zama Mncwango

Keep moving

No matter how dark it may get

Keep moving

No matter how tired you may feel

Keep moving

No matter what people may say about you

Keep moving

No matter your friends or family turning their
back on you or even backstabbing you

Keep moving

No matter what people think of you

Keep moving

Even when people laugh at your pain

Keep moving

Even when you feel like throwing in the towel, do
not

Keep moving

You are almost there

Keep moving

Your morning is coming

Keep moving

Keep trusting in Him

Hold on

You are a winner

You are a conqueror

Victory is yours

6. <u>THE BEST NEWS EVER</u>

*And I will do whatever you ask in my name,
so that the Father may be glorified in the Son.*

*You may ask me for anything in my name, and
I will do*

John 14: 13-14

Words of Inspiration

We asked God for our son to breath on his own without the oxygen pipes and He answered.

We asked God for our son to be discharged from ICU and he was discharged.

He experienced the negligence of two nurses, the infection but God carried him through it all and He answered our prayers and our son was discharged.

Whatever you are asking God for, He will answer.

Have faith and continue to pray,

your miracle is on the way.

In His word, He says that when two or more are gathered in my name, I will be there. Keep praying and trust Him.

The following day and weeks, the experiment to have him breathing independently continued. Manqoba was coping, until he was taken off the oxygen pipes permanently. When the doctor told me that, there is no need to keep him in the hospital since he could breathe without the help of the machine, he was ready to be discharged. The best news ever… I was so thrilled and relieved. I called and informed his dad about the best news and that he has been discharged. We went home to get his clothes and all the necessities, all happiness and smiles.

It was around 5pm-5:30pm when he was discharged. I was overjoyed to have my baby come home, home where he belongs. It took one month and eleven days since his birth. All the glory be unto to God, He answered our prayers.

Our testimony is "there is power in prayer!"

I remember just how we would pray daily. When we visited him at the hospital, I would hold his one hand and his dad held the other hand. We would pray and declare that he is healed and will come home to be with us. At home, with my daughter and his dad, it was a routine where we each took his clothes and blankets and prayed over them and declared his healing and spoke positive affirmations. We spoke life, growth, progress, healing, full recovery, success, all the good things we believed God for about his life. We steadfastly prayed and that helped us remain focused. Our faith increased and was strengthened. We believed in the power of prayer more than anything.

I would sometimes take his blanket with to the hospital, even though we are not permitted in the ward to bring a blanket, I just believed this would also help him. Only in ward 66, they would let us get away with it, it's like they knew how this comforted us as parents. In ICU, you could not break the rules, it was not allowed.

I would wrap him around with his blanket. It became my routine to wrap him up with his blanket which we had been praying over. This I did until the day he was discharged. All this, taught us and confirmed that God indeed works in mysterious ways. It reminded me of God's promise that His ways are higher than our ways, His thoughts are not our thoughts. He is able to do exceedingly, abundantly, above, all we could ask or imagine. All we needed to do was to keep our faith locked in Him, He definitely answered our prayers.

Home sweet home

On the 20th of April 2018, Manqoba came home. My son was home. This was the moment I was looking forward to since his birth. This was the day I always was yearning to see. I was always hopeful that this day would come, and it was finally here. We were all so happy, big sister was more ecstatic, because it was her first time seeing him live, she had only seen him from the photos we took of him in the hospital. She was not allowed to visit in the ICU and the ward. Only us as parents and the grandparents were allowed for visits. The strict rules for infection control and well-being of the babies had to be observed.

I remember one day, my sister wanted to visit Manqoba at the hospital, we had to pretend that she was the grandmother. What could I do, it was comforting to have her come. I could do with her support.

Now that my son was home, it was delightful yet scary because there were no hospital staff at home. We were very cautious but enjoyed the experience.

° **Another battle to face**

Manqoba was about 5 days at home since he was discharged from the hospital. This one evening after his dad left, before we went to bed, I checked up on Manqoba and realised his face was turning blue in colour. I called out his name, he didn't seem to be breathing nor responding. I gently hit him on his back trying to wake him up, he was still not responding. Petrified, I woke my daughter up to alert her about Manqoba and I ran outside to our neighbour to ask for help, by then he was breathing but I still asked that they take us to a nearby hospital urgently so they can attend to him.

We were taken to the hospital as soon as we could, took all the files with. I recall my daughter giving me my sleeping gown, only then I realised I was running around only in my underwear and vest. Can you believe it? I had a serious matter to attend to here and didn't even realize that I was not dressed appropriately.

On arrival at the hospital, I explained what had happened and they looked into his file. They examined him and I was told that he was fine, this is something that happens to babies born prematurely. It was said premature babies can forget to breathe sometimes. It's normal and expected. I did not know that! What a surprise! This journey is full of new discoveries.

The following morning, my boy was fine, however, a day later, I noticed his one shoulder and knee were swollen. I thought maybe we had let him sleep on one side for long. I would massage him gently with a warm cloth and rub gently with Vaseline. On the third day, I realized he was not improving, we took him to the doctor who referred us to a private hospital this time.

They admitted him and needed to run some check-ups, scans and x-rays. They realised that the shoulder and knee were swollen, there was fluid, an infection. He needed to be admitted. They said they could not admit him in the normal ward because he was born prematurely and was small in terms of his weight so as a safety precaution, he will be placed in a special ward, in the ICU.

My heart sank, it became heavy because I could not take another admittance, another hospital visit. It was a setback. It seemed like our joy and excitement of having him at home was short lived. My baby had to be admitted again. I could not take it. I wept, I felt disappointed and heart broken. Nevertheless, the doctors assured me that he will be well, just necessary medical procedures and check-ups that needed to be conducted. They discovered he had an infection, apparently an infection a baby can only catch in the labour ward, he needed to be admitted until it was gone.

So, my life was back to hospital visits. The experience in the private hospital was different, actually better. I didn't have to be there the whole day, I could still go back home to rest and come back. It was a different set up, a much better set up for him and for myself. He had an excellent doctor. All this was comforting on its own.

Complications explained

Whilst Manqoba was still in hospital, the doctor called and asked to see me. My fiancé and I decided to go together. The doctor asked us more and further questions about the records on my son's hospital file. She wanted to know if everything was explained to us about the condition our baby was going through since his birth. We explained what we knew and all that we were told about from the other hospital where he was born. This doctor helped to explain the condition with more clarity and what could be the case for Manqoba's health, I could not believe what the doctor told us.

The bleeding, the complications that comes with the bleeding in his brain, what it could cause to his health. The blood was not circulating correctly in the eye area. They were also worried about his vision due to the bleeding in the brain. He was not a playing baby, like other babies do, his arms were not moving like they should. Because of the bleeding in his brain, we are looking at possibilities of rising a child with disability. She went on explaining all the possibilities of his condition.

It was just unbelievable, that all that the doctor was telling us could be happening to and with our baby. By the time we left the hospital, we were so distressed and heart broken. We left with heavy hearts. Just when we thought life was going to be normal, we were going to live a normal happy family life, another blow that deflated our happiness bubble. I felt numb. I felt stunned. I didn't want to accept and believe that our son might end up disabled.

We had to push harder in prayer, you know when the Bible says, '*The fervent prayer of the righteous availeth much...*' we kept pushing and believing that the 'Impossible is possible with God'.

7. <u>MEN DO GRIEVE, MOST SILENTLY</u>

One day, I will wipe away every tear and take away all your pain

Revelation 21:4

Words of Inspiration

When the going gets tough, remember: Life is tough, but so are you

I think my fiancé seemed to understand better what the doctor was explaining and saying. I, on the other hand, tried to make sense of what all that meant for our son. Personally, at that moment, I refused to believe the doctor's report about our son. I did not want to accept such a report to be factual. I rejected it and denied to believe the possibilities of our son living with any disability.

You know, for the first time since this whole ordeal, I saw my fiancé cry. We were sitting in the car, parked outside where I stayed at that time, he started talking, repeating what the doctor had told us and how disappointed he was feeling, tears fell down his cheeks. He was telling me about the plans he had for our son and now this. I knew he had taken a lot over time and since the birth of our son. He broke down, it was now too much to contain himself. He needed to release the pain, the worry, the stress, the fear, the burden and the undesirable possibilities. It was like the reality we were praying against has come to confront us.

My fiancé had, had to be strong for all of us and denied himself to go through emotions that came with all the setbacks we experienced and our son had to endure in hospital. It was an emotional roller coaster.

Often it's like men are expected to postpone their tears in order to be strong for others who are in more pain. A calm demeanor does not mean a man is in denial any more than tears mean he is emotionally unstable. There is no need to be ashamed of tears, for tears bore witness that a man had the greatest of courage, the courage to suffer.

Many men are still not comfortable with the idea of crying, especially in front of someone. Men don't naturally cry less than women. Societal pressures begin to creep in. Men have heard messages such as:

- "Be tough"
- "Be a man"
- "Don't be weak"
- "Crying is for wimps"
- "Always be strong. Don't cry"

Men in general, feel a lot of pressure, and are always perceived as the strong one in relationships. From a very early age, as boys, they are taught to just suck it up and move on, and if they express their emotions, they may get teased and bullied. So men grow up thinking that if they cry, it means they are less of a man.

Tears are not a sign of weakness, though. Tears are quite the opposite, a sign of strength, love and trust. Men who are able to access their emotions can do so because they are confident of their masculinity and feel comfortable in front of the woman who they are crying to. In a relationship, there should be a safe space where both of you can let your guards down and become completely vulnerable. It would be a very bad sign for a relationship if one or both people don't feel comfortable enough to open up to the other.

Men generally process and respond to their grief very privately and actively, they like to keep busy. You may not see the occasions where they do cry just like you do, they feel the pain just as much, but express it in different ways – they still hurt.

In our case, I realised it was a moment of mind-fullness to show the power of living in the moment, embracing his current circumstances without judgement or pretence. I needed to also allow my fiancé to go through and express his emotions the best way he could without judging him. He has been through a lot himself, in his own way. I understood his feeling of pain and fear, and I thought the tears were completely warranted.

8. <u>FROM DADDY'S POINT OF VIEW</u>

But as many as received Him, to them He gave the right to become children of God, to those who believe in His name

John 1:12

No child or parent should have to beg to be in each other's life ...

Finding out that I will be a dad

When I found out that we were expectant, I was excited, knowing that a child is a blessing and a gift from God. I was filled with excitement that I am going to have a baby, even though I didn't know the gender of the baby, I was hoping it will be a son, an heir.

When we went to the gynaecologist for check-up and scan, we learnt that we were going to have a baby boy…. WOW, I literally saw stars. I was elated. Not that I did not want a baby girl, but a son. I was looking forward to having a son with my fiancée.

The other day, we went to Vaal, I remember my fiancée, Zama, was not feeling well. We went to a local clinic for check-up and we were told everything is fine. I took her back home so she can rest. An hour late she called me, telling me she needed to be rushed to hospital because she thinks she might be in labour, so I had to arrange an employee of mine to take her to hospital.

What scared me the most was that it was not yet time, it was still seven months. I was scared, I was thinking many things. Nonetheless, MY SON was born, yes, a premature. He looked so tiny inside that machine. He was so tiny.

Emotions I experienced

I was petrified, seeing his tiny body with all the drips and tubes, but remained hopeful that my son will make it. I fell in love with him. I asked to pick him up, and we prayed for him. I only asked God for life over his body, but also strength to go through all this. There were times I also felt that we might lose him because other people when we explained his condition to them, they were not optimistic. It sometimes looked unpromising. We also would hear many other horrible stories about how babies die in that hospital, on weekends. This did not make it easy at all.

Men have feelings too, they just express them differently

People have the preconceived notion that men simply do not have feelings. This is far from the case. The problem is in the fact that women believe men should feel things the way they do. The truth is that men have a much harder time processing these feelings. Men are taught from an early age that they need to be strong, confident and apathetic. They begin to equate emotions with weakness.

Societal expectations have "taught" men not to display any emotions. This becomes a huge problem in relationships because men suppress their feelings since they tend not to have socially acceptable emotional outlets. They do not want to seem "emasculated" for caring about someone or something on a deeper level.

It is obvious that men and women differ in the way they each express their emotions, but the difference is how they outwardly express and react to them. Scientifically, it has been proven that men tend to use the left side of their brain, which is where reasoning lies, whereas women tend to use the right side of their brain, which is attributed to emotion. This is what gives women the greater ability to comprehend people and express their emotions more efficiently.

"Emotions live in the background of a man's life and the foreground of a woman's."

Societal norms really seem to be the driving force for this "phenomenon." The different ways men and women display their emotions can cause a lot of confusion when they communicate with one another. It is imperative that we make ourselves aware of these differences, so that we are able to converse more successfully, while building relationships with other people.

Masculinity and emotion...

It is important for men to be able to show their emotions for two distinct reasons: for the health and the well-being of their relationships, and for their own personal health and well-being.

Firstly, the ability to express emotions will help a man resolve issues with their partner. You don't have to guess what your partner is thinking more times than you can count, and it can be frustrating. Being in a relationship makes you want to help your partner; you want to be able to take care of them and help them through the hard times. If your partner is not able to show his feelings though, how can you know just where his mind is at, how can you know what is bothering him?

Secondly, men need to be able to admit their emotions in case they have anxiety or depression, which can only be identified and treated if they own that they have something they need to deal with.

The point is men tend to show anger and women show sadness. But if a man is sad, he should be able to express it, if he has depression, he should be able to get help.

As a partner, a friend or family member, it is important to recognize when a man in your life is hurting and let him know it's OK for him to express those emotions. Show them you love them by supporting them through the lows, not just the highs, of life.

9. <u>MANQOBA IS AN OVERCOMER</u>

We are more than conqueror through Him who loved us

Romans 8:37

Words of Inspiration

We fall. We break. We fail... BUT then, we rise, we heal, we overcome.

After some time, I could notice that my son's condition was improving, I had to be strong for my fiancée and for him. Prayer kept us strong, it kept us going. The baby was gaining weight, showing all positive signs. The doctors report was good, we were encouraged. We were so hopeful that sooner he will be discharged and come home.

The other day, he was taken for full examination and we waited for the results. The doctor was not happy with his heart condition. Since he was born prematurely, his heart was not fully developed, there is a hole and it was slowing the full recovery process. We were told that it is something we should not worry about, if it does not close by itself naturally, he can undergo an operation.

The following day when I went to visit him, my fiancée, Zama noticed that his belly button looked weird, it looked swollen and she showed the nurse, who said it's natural and common. Yet the results confirmed he had an infection. He was taken back to ICU.

When he was taken back to ICU, the feeling I would have was unsettling. ICU is like a matter of life or death. It's traumatising. I decided to keep quiet, I don't like to complain at times. I believed I needed to be strong for both my partner and our son. I kept believing he will fine, he was in capable hands of doctors.

My son was discharged from ICU and put in a normal ward. Then days went by, and eventually the doctors were happy with his progress and decided to discharge him. When we went to collect his medication, we discovered his file had documents missing with valuable information which again was negligence. They tried to sort it out with the help of information that Zama gave them and was able to discharge him.

We took our son home FINALLY…. We were grateful to God for this milestone.

Few days later, he developed an infection on his shoulder and knee and realized it was not getting better. We took him to a local GP just to have him checked. The doctor recommended that we take him to the hospital. We took him to a nearby hospital because we were no longer happy with the previous one. After all the hassles, the doctor confirmed it's a serious condition, the case needs a specialist, my boy needs to be admitted.

Oh no, that meant we needed to go through the same experience once again. Anyway, he was admitted and was put on treatment. We visited him daily. The doctor, after running many tests, called us for a 'serious talk' and she explained to us the condition of our son, from the bleeding in the head which would lead to disability, the worry about his vision because of the bleeding in the head, infection in his knee and shoulder and what it could do to his joints especially the knee.

I was shocked, scared, BUT I didn't show Zama because I thought I must hide my emotions.

You know when you were looking forward to a gift, a son and the next thing you are told he might not be as perfect. My mind began to race everywhere. I began thinking of how it would change our lives; the daily challenges of raising a child with special needs; it is not easy; I have seen it before. I started seeing all the possibilities and impossibilities of him growing up with those challenges. I was thinking that his development will be slow and not reach milestones at the appropriate time. Nonetheless, we trusted God about everything.

The reality was that I wanted a child, a son who is fine, not who has a disability. I didn't know what to do, except pray to God about it. We will have to learn to love, support and raise the baby together. I had to accept the situation, if it was God's will, then let it be.

After spending some time in the hospital, my boy was recovering well. He was picking up weight, he was getting stronger, he was looking fine. The bleeding had stopped. My boy was taken to an eye specialist also, they confirmed he will be able to see properly.

On the day, we were meant to fetch him, for him to be discharged, I was so excited to hold him and take him home. Since then, he has been improving, he is doing well. He is a fighter, a real lion. He has overcome!

I would say to my boy, he must continue to fight because one day we won't be around to fight for him. He is a little warrior, a conqueror. I desire best things for him, that he must be the best of the best.

As men, we must not shift more responsibility to women. Men must give support, make it a point that you don't show your weaknesses to your partner, because you can't both be weak.

Communication is more important, praying together, visiting together. Prayer is the essence that kept us going and made all of us to overcome. As partners, stick together and be strong for one another.

10. <u>A MESSAGE OF COMFORT</u>

Be strong and courageous, do not be afraid or tremble at them, for the Lord your God is the one who goes with you, He will not fail you or forsake you

Deuteronomy 31:6

Words of Inspiration

Great things never come from comfort zones.

This is a message of comfort dedicated to parents who have a child, sick in hospital

You are still there, aren't you? You are still at the hospital waiting for results, for your child to wake up, and for any glimpse of good news; anything that will settle your heart to the hope of a new day without sickness. You are tired, but you do not want to show it. You put on a strong face, but you wonder sometimes if you can keep this costume of strength on.

You have found yourself to be a superhero of sorts. During those quiet moments, you feel like Clark Kent. You feel vulnerable, weak, and absolutely human. Yet, during those strong moments where your sick child is watching, you adorn yourself with that cape of strength that you have uncomfortably worn for a while now. You become Superman. You stay up all night thinking about the monitors next to your child. You make a list of questions for treatment options, expectations and possibilities. That brave mask you wear that shows no sign of weakness or vulnerability is rarely taken off, especially around your partner and your sick child.

Yet, you sneak off to the isolated corners of the hospital where no one can see you. You weep with the agony of a desperate heart. You cry out, *"Please, please. Heal my child."* You bargain with God. You tell Him that you would gladly trade positions with your child. You would shorten your life in order to lengthen the life of your baby. *You, dear parent of a sick child, are a weary soldier.*

It is okay for you to weep in the quiet corners of the hospital, and to bargain about extending your child's life. It is okay for you to yearn to swap places with your sick child. You are only human, you know. But…

You are a warrior. You hold your child with an incomparable measure of strength as he or she gets one more treatment, one more injection that cannot seem to find a vein, and one more painful test. You stay up all night in order to catch your child opening his or her eyes for the first time in several weeks.

Your shield has become one of hope. It may get dings in it, but you never stop carrying it. It has become your defensive weapon against those who bring you bad news. Although dampened at times, it still reflects a light that others catch when around you.

You are one of the toughest kind of parents. You are a survivor of a war waged on the one person you would give your life for. You did not ask for this. You did not expect this. You were barely able to stand when you received the news that broke your heart, but, you stood for your child.

Yes, you are a Superhero of sorts. You are a warrior. You wear the mask of bravery, the cape of strength, and the shield of hope.

Do you want to know something?

Your child knows you are there. Your child sees your brave face. Your child does not know that you disappear to the isolated corners of the hospital. Your child does not realize that your knees buckled at the devastating news. Your child also does not know that you bargain with God on his or her behalf.

Do you want to know why?

Because while you are busy being a non-glorified superhero, you step aside so that your child becomes the warrior, the fighter, and the one who receives the praise for being strong.

Your kind of strength only comes around every so often. Most parents will (thankfully) never know the depths of exhaustion mixed with a sliver of hope that you have gone through.

Sneak off to the quiet corners of the hospital if you need to. Pray, and plead with God about the life of your child. Advocate for treatment options, keep your mask of bravery, cape of strength, and shield of hope on.

For your child…

the one you pray over

the one you bargain for

the one your knees buckled in despair over

the one you put on a mask of bravery for

the one you wear your cape of strength around, and

the one you carry your shield of hope for

will also wear a mask of bravery, a cape of strength, and a shield of hope.

Dear Parent of a sick child, you are a warrior.

11. <u>THE DAUGHTER, THE BIG SISTER</u>

God is our refuge and strength, a very present help in times of trouble. Therefore, we will not fear

Psalm 46:1-2

Words of Inspiration

Great works are performed, not by strength but by perseverance

I am Nokukhanya, Manqoba's big sister, I am just a friendly and warm young lady who loves life and being with her friends. I have gotten used to and enjoyed life as the ONLY child in the house for some years. I lived my life as an ordinary girl.

I remember when my mom told me that she is pregnant, I was excited about the news because I always desired to have a sibling, especially a little sister so I can play with and spend time together, doing girlish stuff together. It did not even bother me that the age gap might come as a challenge, what I was looking forward to was having somebody who will look up to me as their big sister.

My mother's pregnancy journey brought some changes in our lives. I had come to learn that pregnancy can change your life, it requires a mind shift so you can prepare yourself emotionally and mentally for the arrival of the baby. It can develop your character because the thought of knowing there is a new member of the family we are expecting, you always need to think how life will be once they are born.

Once the baby's gender was confirmed, I was not disappointed that I will be having a baby brother, instead, I started having many ideas about the things that I will be doing with him as he grows up. I could imagine the two of us playing together, spending time in our room, visiting interesting places and creating fun and awesome memories.

Admiration for my mom

I watched and observed as my mom adjusted to a pregnant woman. She looked after herself. She knew she was carrying a special gift from God. It was God's favour upon her life. I watched as she daily ensured all was well with her and the baby. What a privilege it is, knowing you are carrying life inside of you, makes you change your priorities. You turn to live for the expectant baby, you start changing your own life to ensure the life you carry is well protected and nurtured.

This journey showed me the other side of my mom that I had not yet known. She is a strong woman, she is a prayerful woman, she carried herself with dignity. *"Uyi-Mbokodo"*, SHE IS A ROCK, and I admire those qualities in her. I realised she is a good role model and I am proud to call her MY mom.

And then, mommy went to hospital to have a baby

I remember the day my mom went to the hospital to have the baby, it was an unplanned incident. It was still early, it was not the expected time, it meant the baby would be born prematurely. She was rushed to the hospital. When I learnt that she gave birth, I was overjoyed, only to find out that it was short-lived because she did not come back home with the baby, I mean, with my baby brother.

So many questions were going through my mind, I was scared, worried not sure what to make of the situation. This was supposed to be the most exciting day in our family. What could have happened? I could see my mom's face was not happy at all. I was also worried about her, what she was going through at the time, but I needed to wait until she explained what was going on.

My baby brother was born prematurely, this meant he needed to be hospitalised, they needed to keep him in ICU to help him develop fully. This might take long. I was so looking forward to meeting my baby brother. I was deeply saddened, but at the same time needed to be strong for my mom.

Visits to the hospital

This was the most difficult time, seeing my mom daily going to visit uManqoba and I could not because I was not allowed into the ward as per hospital policies. I had not had the opportunity to meet my own little brother. I could only imagine how he looked, what he would be doing, what he was going through and unfortunately could not be there for him, to assure him that all will be well.

Prayer kept me strong, it kept me grounded and helped me to remain positive about the whole situation. Many times I could see and hear my mom pray and that would also encourage me. It was a tough period for me, and for my mom of course.

These hospital visits lasted forever. Every time my mom will come back with a 'not-so-good' report, my heart would sink. I began to wonder if my baby brother will ever come home. He has not been home, I have not met him. I was not aware that emotionally this whole situation was starting to wear me off. My performance at school began to drop, I didn't want to be home and wait for another bad report from the doctors.

To escape and manage all that was happening, I started hanging out more with my friends, just to take my mind off my reality at home. To try and take my mind off possibilities of things not going the way we have been praying. Unfortunately, this also did not make it easy for my mom, she was not happy with my conduct. There was a strain to our relationship and I didn't mean to add more stress for my mom.

Manqoba is coming home

Did I hear correctly? My baby brother is coming home… I was over the moon; I was more than excited! I had prayed and longed for this day, it felt like many years. You can imagine many things going on in my mind. The day has finally arrived!

I will never forget the smile on my mom's face when she arrived. I couldn't wait to introduce myself to my baby brother. I was not sure exactly what to do with myself. Holding him for the first time, starring at him, hoping he'd open his eyes to meet mine, I carried his little body and felt the connection right there. Welcome home champ! Welcome home, where you belong.

I learnt so much about myself

This whole journey has helped me understand myself better. I didn't know I can stand in the gap in prayer for somebody else. I learnt that there will be times when I have to think of others first, their needs above mine. Above all, I learnt that tough times bring out the best in us when we remain hopeful and positive. I learnt that nothing is impossible with God, only if we believe. God answers prayer, we must just wait on His timing.

My mom, my role model, my rock

I would like to say that my mom is the best in the world. She is a woman of integrity. She is a woman of stature. She is brave, she is bold, she is strong. She is victorious and I am proud of her. I am proud of the woman she has become. I am proud to be her daughter. I am happy she is in my life.

12. <u>MANQOBA'S GOING FOR AN OPERATION –THE LAST LEG</u>

Even though I walk through the darkest valley, I will fear no evil, for you are with me, your rod and your staff, they comfort me

Psalm 23:4

Words of Inspiration

For desperate time, put your faith in God. For hopeless times, require His strength. For bleak times, require His grace. For troubling times, let prayer surround you.

'The last leg'

The time had finally come for Manqoba to do the small operation, after eleven months and two weeks of living, breathing and playing as a child whilst having a hole in his heart. The date was set, 25th February 2019.

I was scared yet hopeful that God will carry us through this challenge again. I had a call from one of the doctors from the hospital which Manqoba was supposed to go to, for the operation. She was calling to tell me that, they have an earlier date available on which they can do this procedure, if I agree. I said, No, I refused to take that earlier date and my reason was because the doctor that checked my son on his last appointment did not explain everything to me about the procedure. I explained my concerns to the doctor I was talking to, on the phone. She asked that we set a day /appointment where I can come in, to have her explain everything to me properly. We agreed on the day, which was the following Wednesday.

The day came and I went to the hospital to see the doctor as we had agreed. When I got there, she was still busy with a patient but the professor who is the main person that will be leading the procedure on the day was available. She called me and asked to explain the whole procedure to me and I said yes. We sat down she took a piece of paper and a pen and started drawing, as she was drawing, she was also explaining every detail of this procedure. By the time she was done, I had a full and clear picture of what was going to take place on the day of the procedure.

As a concerned parent I took it upon myself to have a second opinion after the doctor who saw Manqoba on the last appointment failed to explain everything concerning the procedure. This was an appointment I had made weeks before I even went to see the professor.

It was on the same week I had gone to see the professor but on a different day which was Friday at 3:30pm. I thought it won't hurt anyone to still go see the cardio specialist and hear what he says as second opinion before we go ahead with the operation. We went into his office, and I gave him my son's file and started explain why we came to see him and what our concerns were, he checked him and also did an echo checkup on him, when all was done he said; he knows the professor because he was taught by her and if there is anyone who can do this procedure it's her, he trusts the procedure will be a success. Should it be that due to anything they decided not to continue with the procedure on the day and they decided to do the full operation, then we don't have to wait, we can just ask the professor to refer us to him for the operation. So, we left his room, relieved and sure as parents of what decision was the right one for our son.

The 22nd of February 2019 came and I took him to the hospital for the blood tests and other check-ups the doctors wanted to do before the procedure, after all the necessities they sat me down and explained again what they were going to do, on the day of the procedure including explaining the complications that could happen on the day. Hmmm, the word "Complication" made me scared, really scared, but, I had to take a leap of faith once again and just TRUST God with my son's life. She explained the complications:

1. He could bleed during the procedure and have to get blood afterwards.

2. His feet could become cold during the procedure but there is antibiotics which helps for that.

3. His heart can slow down during the procedure and have to resuscitate him.

4. He could die on the table because like any procedure anything could happen.

Iyoo, that one terrified me a lot, but I signed the papers and gave them permission to go ahead with the procedure, I trust you Lord, I trust you, that's what I kept saying in my heart, I had to focus on the positive side of this procedure. We finally got finished and left the hospital and went back home.

Sunday, was the day my baby was going to be admitted to hospital for this procedure, I prepared everything I thought he would need and we drove to hospital. We arrived at the ward and did all the paper work for him to be admitted, the doctor who was going to put him to sleep came and explained her part of what she will be doing and there after I stayed with him till around 7pm because I wanted to leave when he was asleep, I then called his dad to came fetch me.

The big day came, Monday, 25th of February 2019, the day of the procedure. I arrived at the hospital just before 7am, he was awake already and that was no surprise, Manqoba is an early bird. My worry was, there were two other babies, a little older than my son who had to undergo the same procedure on that day, who will be first? Mind you, my son has not eaten since yesterday around 9pm, when the nurse tried to feed him his formula at 12 mid-night as his last meal before the procedure, she says; he was crying and did not want to drink his formula. So, I just hoped he would be the first to do the procedure. I waited patiently, for the guy to come and fetch one of the babies, finally at 08:05am he came and called out Manqoba's name. I was happy, that he was the first one to undergo the procedure. I walked by his side as the guy pushed the stretch bed which he was lying in, we arrived outside the theatre-room and waited a little.

Finally, they called us into the theatre room, me and my son, I picked him-up and entered the room, by that time it was 08:30am. Wow, I looked around and was stunned, my first time entering the theatre-room, it was so real. My heart started beating fast, they asked me to sit down with my son. The one lady asked to check his Blood Pressure while the other gentleman explained what was going to happen next. All the doctors arrived including the professor and everyone else. They marked the register, everyone was present. This was a team of about 15 people in one room" theatre" who all had an important role to play in this procedure. They then told me; they are going to put my son to sleep so that the procedure can start. They asked me to put him on the table and IMMEDIATELY they put a mask over his nose and in just few seconds he was out, I was then asked to wait outside until they were done.

I waited outside, the time was 08:45am and the first thing I did was to call his father 'Bheki' and tell him the procedure had started. He suggested I come to his office which was about 10 minutes away, just so I do not have to think too much while I waited but I could not leave the hospital, the doctors needed me there until the end of the procedure. I explained that to my partner and he understood. I then called my father, my spiritual brother and my two spiritual mothers to carry me in prayer as the procedure had started. As I continued to sit outside the theatre room, I put on my headphones so I can listen to gospel music on my phone, this helped me not to think too much instead it calmed me down. At 10:10am, a lady came with a smile on her face and told me, the doctor wanted to see me. As we were walking in the passage, the doctor met me halfway to tell me the good news. I think she was so excited she could not wait those few seconds for me to come to her inside the theatre room, so she could tell me the good news.

We went inside the room and everyone was smiling and happy in the room. I had never seen anything like that, I sat down and she showed me the pictures in the computer, before and after the procedure and explained everything. I cried, it was tears of joy, I was so happy and thrilled that all went well. I thanked the doctor and the rest of her team. She gave me the teddy bear from the company where they get the 'stopper' which they use to close the hole with. That will be a souvenir I will keep for Manqoba.

My son had conquered once again, all the glory be unto God. I called his father and everyone I had called before the procedure to let them know, all was well. We conquered through prayer once again. There were no complications, not even one. That same day when he was back in the ward, it was as if nothing had happened, he was playing as usual. For safety purpose, he stayed in hospital till Wednesday around lunch time, the doctors just wanted to make sure all was well. He was then discharged after his check-up was done, all the other necessities were done also, we passed by his father's work place so he can see his son, then went home.

Manqoba Smangaliso Shabangu, my handsome, adorable son has been doing well ever since the procedure. He is growing stronger and stronger every day, so full of life and lots of energy. He is still on the heart medication till June. The doctors will then decide if he stops the medication or not, I am hopeful he is soon to stop the medication.

Where to from here?

This has been a journey and a half, all worth it. Perhaps will have part two or even part three of this book, written by him, uManqoba. Only time will tell, right now I'm enjoying motherhood. I love spending time with him every day, playing with him, hearing his laugher, feeding him, bathing him, every moment is very special to me. The time he started to sit on his own, him crawling, learning to stand and now learning to walk, it can only be God.

This was not an easy journey but a journey worth taking.

13. <u>AN ATTITUDE OF GRATITUDE</u>

Oh give thanks unto the Lord for He is good, for His mercy endures forever

Psalm 136:1

He who began a good work in you, will carry it into completion – Phil.1:6

Gratitude always unlocks the fullness of life. It adds meaning to our being and makes sense of what lies ahead of us. Looking back at 2018 with a heart full of gratitude. It was an amazing year of learning the new and unlearning the old, of some incredible people, experiences and memories.

What does it mean to 'have an attitude of gratitude?' What is gratitude? How can gratitude change your life?

Gratitude to me is being grateful and thankful for everything in your life. This includes the people in your life, the lessons and challenges in your life, the things that bring you joy and comfort, the basic necessities of life. It means not taking anything for granted and accepting and appreciating what you have and who you are right now.

Having an attitude of gratitude shifts your awareness from what you are lacking to the abundance that you already possess. Practicing gratitude acknowledges all of the blessings in your life.

An attitude of gratitude is not naturally easy during times of great difficulty, but cultivating a gratitude attitude is a sure way to secure the help if God for your release from the predicaments of life.

This is why I would sincerely love to express my heartfelt appreciation and gratitude to the following special people who all had a role to play in my journey.

I would like to thank the following key role players in this journey

- ✓ Doctors in children's ICU and the cardio doctors from the Hospital
- ✓ Manqoba's pediatrician
- ✓ My family, especially sister Nammy
- ✓ My spiritual brother - Lucky Rivimbi
- ✓ My spiritual sister - Tumelo Nkosi
- ✓ oMama bom'khuleko'women/mother's of prayer' who come to my show on Thursdays

They carried me with prayer, they would call regularly to lift me up with God's word at times they would pray with me over the phone and that would strengthen me and also my colleagues support.

May God work all those things that seem impossible in your lives to be possible.

Ngiyabonga kakhulu- Thank you very much …

AS I SAY A PRAYER

Heavenly Father, thank you for your faithfulness. I believe that you are working behind the scenes even when I cannot see it. I choose to keep believing. I choose to look again until I see every promise fulfilled in Jesus name.

Whatever trials, whatever tribulations are placed at my feet, thank you for always being there, to pick me up, turn me around, restore me and make me whole.

Dear Lord, as I thank you for the gift of life, I also thank you for the gift of wonderful people I have met along this journey. Some of them inspire me, stretch me, challenge me, love me and encourage me. All of them helped me to realize how meaningful and beautiful my life is. I love them so much. Bless them Lord with good health, security, wealth, success, peace, joy and love. Grant them their prayers too.

I am complete in your boundless love as I walk in your never-ending grace. Thank you, Lord in Jesus name... Amen

I thank God for blessing me with you guys, you are so special to me and I love you so much. I cherish every moment spent with you, my darlings. May the good Lord keep you safe and continue to bless you guys.

Mncwa, mncwa, mncwa 'kiss'.